waves

waves

SARA MARGHERITA
CASSUOLI DAVIDE

Life Rattle Press Toronto

Cover Design, Typeset and Illustrations
by Sara Margherita Cassuoli Davide

Copyedited by Adelaide Clare Attard

Published in Canada by Life Rattle Press

Life Rattle New Publishers Series
ISSN 978-1-897161-84-5

ISBN 978-1-989861-10-3

Library and Archives Canada Cataloguing in Publication

Title: Waves / Sara Margherita Cassuoli Davide.
Names: Cassuoli Davide, Sara Margherita, 1997- author.
Description: Series statement: Life Rattle new publishers series, 1713-8981
Identifiers: Canadiana 20200208454 | ISBN 9781989861103 (softcover)
Subjects: LCSH: Cassuoli Davide, Sara Margherita, 1997-—Family. | LCSH:
Authors, Canadian—21st
    century—Biography. | CSH: Authors, Canadian (English)—21st Century—Bi-
ography. | CSH: Italian
    Canadians—Biography.
Classification: LCC PS8605.A87 Z46 2020 | DDC C811/.6—dc23

To The Ones No Longer Here

CONTENTS

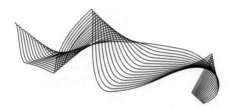

prologue

DEATH AND GRIEF ARE EXPERIENCES THAT AFFECT EVERYONE.

Someone in your life will die. Although it's something we don't like to think about, death is inevitable.

Grief is a universal experience yet grieving often looks different for each person. That doesn't stop people from trying to explain the process, though.

They say grief comes in waves. That explanation resonates with me most and reflects my experience with grief.

I'm on a boat, and it's shaky, but fine for the most part; yet, waves of grief crash onto me. Then, at other times, the water is still.

I've tried to anchor myself, but, inevitably, these emotions and trauma come to the surface.

Grief demands to be felt.

I held my dad's, Papá's, hand when he died unexpectedly in 2016.

In 2017, my sister Chiara died when I turned my back on her and went to greet our family members in her hospice room.

In 2019, my family and I were chanting *Ave Maria* to my grandmother, Nonna Vittoria, when she passed away.

Before this concentration of losses, my grief was a ripple oscillating below water. It was dormant, but it was there.

Both my grandfathers died when I was eight years old.

In 2005, Nonno Carlo had a heart attack and died. A few months later, Nonno Peppe caught pneumonia that mixed fatally with his cancer.

I realize now that the grieving of my sister started in 2007.

My ripple of grief gradually grew when I was ten years old, as I watched her body shut down for ten years.

I experienced grief for half of my existence.

Grief can live outside of death, but with my experience of grief, they are housed together, intertwined in their existence. One is not one without the other.

With each death, I experienced grief differently, yet one fact remained the same—I always glossed over it.

When I was eleven years old, I cried in a theatre watching Miley Cyrus's hybrid documentary and concert movie. She talked about her grandfather's death. Although years later, that was the first time that I truly thought about the deaths of my grandfathers.

Though I've grown and experienced more grief since crying in the theatre, the way I've dealt with grief and trauma throughout the years seem to remain the same—I don't.

I didn't understand the deaths of my grandfathers. I didn't understand my grief.

I thought it was because of my young age, but their deaths became a pattern of how I grieve—I rob myself of the right to.

I grew up in an Italian Roman Catholic household. I went to St.

Fidelis Elementary School. I prayed every night, said grace before meals, and went to church for every religious event.

When I went to Etobicoke School of the Arts for high school, I had a falling out with Catholicism. I had a break for five years until I had to go back to church for Papá's funeral.

As people in my family continued to die, I had to go back to church and face a religion that was dead to me. A place that was comforting years prior was now filled with anxiety, uneasiness, and funeral services.

The deaths of Papá, Chiara, and Nonna Vittoria brought on a forced exploration of faith. The question of where someone goes when they die is one that I've been forced to think about. My answer changes every day.

Grief comes to the surface in this collection of personal essays, short stories, and poetry. These pieces are a retelling of the events that turned my tempestuous waters into waves.

STORIES

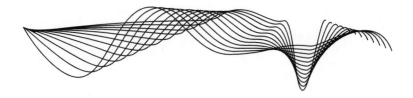

papá

papá

I WAS EIGHTEEN YEARS OLD WHEN PAPÁ DIED SUDDENLY.

I knew my sister was dying, even though my family held on to the belief that she would miraculously fight her undiagnosed illness—my parents bringing her to specialists overseas, my mom buying every alternative healing tool she could afford.

I accepted the inevitability of her death.

I didn't expect my dad to die.

Papá's prostate cancer made an aggressive comeback after being in remission for ten years. It spread to the rest of his organs, fast-tracking his death.

I was living in Montreal, starting my first year at Concordia University, when Papá was re-diagnosed. A few months into the first semester, Mom called me to tell me that Papá was back in Rome for his scheduled treatment and check-up.

Last check-up, Papá was given chemotherapy in the form of pills and had to go to Rome every three months to keep an eye on the effectiveness of the pills.

Mom and Papá met in Rome, but despite marrying Mom, a Canadian citizen, he didn't want to give up his Italian citizenship.

We all lived in Rome for the first few years of my life. When I was four, Mom, Chiara, and I moved to Toronto and Papá stayed in Rome for work.

Because of Papá's citizenship status, he couldn't access health-care in Toronto and needed to fly back to Rome for his checkups.

Before Mom, Papá's life was in Rome. His Italian identity lived strong. When Papá died, I started reading Italian literature. I tried to speak Italian as much as I could. I took classes on Italian culture. All to make my Italian identity as strong as his; for it to live on through me.

When I was in Montreal for school, Mom quit her job and sold our family home on Burr Avenue in Toronto. Papá stayed past his three-month-threshold to help Mom with the move and Chiara's care.

I couldn't be there to help them with the move, so I sent them a care-package—popcorn for Mom and scratch-and-win lottery tickets for Papá.

When Mom, Papá, and Chiara set themselves up in their new home on Patricia Avenue, Papá went back to Rome for his de-layed, scheduled visit.

Papá used to work for *Alitalia* airlines as a ticketing agent and would fly standby to Toronto to visit me, Mom, and Chiara.

I have vivid memories of running through Fiumicino airport in Rome after flying in from Toronto.

An eight-hour plane ride didn't stop a five-year-old girl from having an outpour of energy, running to her dad after not seeing him for months, and jumping into his arms.

Papá would come visit us in Toronto whenever he could. Mom says it was three times a year, but I don't remember Papá being around that much before Chiara got sick.

Papá would fly less often when Chiara got sick, and he moved in with me, Mom, and Chiara in Toronto.

Papá sacrificed his comfort to be close to Chiara during her illness, taking any seat available to not delay his journey to her.

He would often go on the jump-seat, which wasn't an actual seat, but a pull-out seat attached to the wall of the plane near the front; a seat where flight attendants would sit during take-off and landing.

Papá would do these flights often, again, when he had to do his three-month-checkups in Rome.

Papá's friend, Rocco, owned a pizzeria near the Colosseum.

Papá visited Rocco each time he arrived in Rome.

He would go straight from the airport after an eight-hour flight to see his friends, eat pizza, and drink wine.

After flying from Toronto to Rome for his check-up, Papá went to Rocco's pizzeria for the last time.

The next day, Papá was out with his brother, Zio Claudio. Papá fell out of Zio's car because he was too weak to stand.

Zio brought him to the hospital soon after and called Mom to tell her the cancer had spread to his liver, and that we should come and see him as soon as possible.

I was in Montreal when Papá was in his final few months of life.

Before Papá went to Rome, and before Zio Claudio told Mom about Papá's cancer's return, Mom noticed Papá grow weaker.

I didn't see Papá physically and couldn't tell from his voice on our phone calls that his health was declining.

Mom called to tell me that she spoke to Zio Claudio. She said he told her that Papá was sick.

She didn't tell me he was dying.

I asked Mom if I could drop out of university and continue living in Montreal. She told me we needed to go see Papá.

I listened.

After filing the paperwork to drop out of Concordia University, I came back to Toronto and flew to Rome with Mom on Christmas Eve.

PAPÁ WAS STAYING WITH HIS MOM, NONNA RINA, WHEN WE ARRIVED IN ROME.

Mom and I went to Nonna Rina's apartment directly from the airport to see him.

Photos of me, Chiara, Nonno Peppe, and my cousins Giorgia and Federica, filled Nonna Rina's house as we walked through her hallway to meet Papá in her room.

Papá laid in her bed with fine-linen sheets and embroidered pillowcases.

Nonna Rina was a seamstress. Even after retirement, she still fixed clothes for the people in her building.

Papá looked different. His eyes were puffy and glossy. His normally golden skin was dull. His brows were furrowed, and his lips were turned.

Papá had a slight sigh of relief when he saw me and Mom.

Papá told Mom that we didn't need to come to see him. He said he was fine.

He didn't know how serious his condition was.

During the last couple weeks of his life, Papá was adamant about taking photos for his expiring passport. He made me take photos of him on my phone because he was too weak to go get them done. His orange sweater didn't help his pale complexion, and even though he tried to smile, Papá's face was sunken.

Papá thought he was fine.

I walked into Nonna Rina's room, wrapped my arms around Papá, and hugged him tight. He felt bony and cold. He was much skinnier than I remembered him.

I laid myself next to Papá. His sunken eyes met mine.

"*Non bere, non fumare, e non fare droghe,*" he said.

"I won't," I replied.

Him telling me not to drink, smoke, or do drugs sent a shock through my body. Papá struggled with alcohol abuse and it caused turmoil in our relationship. I would get angry when he drank too much. He would shrug it off like it was nothing.

Papá never got violent when he drank, but he and Mom would argue and shout when he did. Papá never got violent when he drank, but it was hard to see him stumble through the house reeking of red wine and cigarettes.

When Papá turned his back to fall asleep, I turned away from him. I let the shock of his comment surge through my body. I tried to silence my weeping. I tried to fall asleep next to him.

When Papá and I woke from our nap, we made our way with Mom to our apartment in Piazzale Jonio—an area just outside of Rome's centre. We held on to Papá as we walked out of Nonna Rina's apartment and into Zio Claudio's Fiat.

We arrived at our apartment where Papá lived without us when receiving treatments, or where he would live and work before Chiara got sick.

When he was still strong enough, Mom and I would roll Papá in his wheelchair down to the Blu Bar Val Melaina, a café below our apartment, next to a jewellery store, bakery, and hot table.

He would order a cappuccino and a croissant *con crema*. I would get a *bomba con crema*, keeping the same lemony-vanilla cream as Papá's croissant, but swapping out the flaky crunch for a sugary dough. Mom would bring cappuccinos in to-go cups and croissants in paper bags for me and Papá when he got too weak to go downstairs.

Papá stayed in my childhood bedroom filled with a wooden bunk bed, green glow-in-the-dark stars on the ceiling, a big-red framed photo of Chiara in a tree with a brown cat when she was seven, and colourful kid's books on the shelf.

I moved the keyboard that was in the apartment hallway into the bedroom and would occasionally play for Papá and his friends when they would come visit.

I SPENT THE FINAL WEEKS OF PAPÁ'S LIFE IN THE TOP BUNK, WHILE PAPÁ SLEPT IN THE BOTTOM.

I was physically there with him, but I felt cold. I was distant. I was numb. I was confused.

I played *Uno* on my iPad, watched *Parks and Recreation* on Netflix, or just sat there in silence.

I remember sitting outside of our apartment near the bus stop, smoking a cigarette, and calling Aunt Nancy.

"I want to come back home," I said. "I want to go back to my life."

I carry the guilt of that feeling to this day.

GRIEF CLOUDED MY RECOLLECTION OF THE MOMENTS THAT I SPENT WITH PAPÁ IN HIS FINAL DAYS.

Right after Papá's death, when I thought about him, I only recalled the moments where I wanted to go home, or the moments that I was physically with him but mentally distant.

As my grief settled, I began to remember the good times, too.

Papá would call me to bring him out on the balcony for a cigarette.

Mom discouraged this, so Papá would always call me instead of her. It was our routine.

I would go to the bunk bed, grab his arms to put him up in a sitting position, lock the wheelchair in place, and lift him off the bed and into the wheelchair.

I would roll him out onto the balcony and leave him outside to smoke.

I hid my own smoking from Papá. I started smoking in the last year of high school. Mom told me that Papá found a pack of my *Belmont Lights*.

He never confronted me about it.

When we were with Papá in Rome, I would say I was going for a walk, go downstairs, and sit in front of the bus stop near our apartment to smoke *Camels*. Papá smoked *Marlboro Reds*. I would come in, wash my hands with hazelnut scented soap, take a swig of mint mouthwash, and pat my face with cold water. During the night, when Papá was asleep, and I ran out of *Camels*, Mom and I would find his old stash of stale cigarettes tucked away in a cupboard in the living room and smoke them on the balcony.

This routine of me bringing Papá out for cigarettes continued when we brought him to San Francesco Caracciolo *Ospizio*, a hospice down the street from our apartment.

I kept bringing him out for smokes until he was too weak to get out of the hospital bed.

Mom slept in the cot we bought from Ikea, and I slept on the extra hospital bed next to Papá.

On the final night of Papá's life, I finished watching Netflix and went to sleep. Mom woke me up in the middle of the night to tell me that she thought Papá had his last breath.

I jumped out of bed and went to hold his hand. He gave one more last breath. I felt like it was for me. He waited until I was there, next to him.

At that moment, I realized how much he cared for me.

I felt his love.

I felt my anguish for him having to die before we could form a stronger bond.

I left Papá's room, stood by the coffee machine, and called my friend Cristina to tell her the news through shaky breaths and yelling cries.

Cristina lost her mother when we were in eighth grade. I knew she would understand.

The people who worked in the hospice picked Papá up from his room two hours later and brought him to the mortuary attached to the hospice. The mortuary acted as a visitation room for Papá's viewing service held on the same day. Everything happened so quickly. Mom and I barely absorbed what was going on.

The harsh January wind and damp air accompanied me and Mom on our walk back to our apartment.

We stopped into Blu Bar Val Melaina on the way and told them the news of Papá's passing.

We waited in our apartment as the hospice workers prepared Papá's body for the viewing.

THE LONG HALLWAY TO ENTER THE MORTUARY, THAT ALSO ACTED AS A VISITATION ROOM, BROUGHT US TO A SMALL CUBICLE SPACE WHERE PAPÁ'S BODY REMAINED ON A COLD, GREY-METAL TABLE.

No other bodies except for Papá's, Mom's and mine, occupied the damp-cement-filled room as we waited for people to come visit Papá.

Papá's body was dressed in a navy suit, and navy tie with a green, orange, and yellow fish pattern on it.

Papá loved to fish. When we were young, he would take me, Mom, and Chiara to Mugnanese—his hometown two hours outside of Rome filled with green rolling hills, sunflower fields, and only fifty residents. He would often bring Chiara on fishing trips with him. Before she got sick.

During the visitation, I kept looking at my phone while sitting in the chair next to Papá's body.

I was reading condolences on Facebook from the post I made about his passing. I had Mom, but I felt like my support system was in Toronto. Or maybe I was scared and couldn't deal with seeing Papá's lifeless body next to me.

The San Francesco Caracciolo *Ospizio* is no longer a hospice. It's called *Casa di Cura* San Francesco Caracciolo. I'm not sure if they actually changed it to a house for cures, or if that makes the place you go to die more enticing.

THE MORNING AFTER THE VISITATION, THE FUNERAL DIRECTOR DROVE ME, MOM, AND PAPÁ'S CASKET TO PORTO, A TOWN JUST OUTSIDE OF MUGNANESE, FOR PAPÁ'S FUNERAL SERVICE.

We sat in the leather seated hearse. The sun peeked through the grey clouds casting a shadow on Papá's casket behind us.

Papá's funeral was the first time that I stepped into a church, since I attended St. Fidelis Elementary School in Toronto, five years prior.

After the funeral service, the funeral directors placed Papá's casket in the crypt in the mausoleum in Porto's outdoor cemetery, overlooking the Umbrian hills.

After everyone left, Zio Claudio, Mom, and I went to the cemetery office and picked out what would be on Papá's crypt.

We settled on an off-white cross that matched the colour of

the frame that held his picture.

When Zio left to drive back into the city, Mom and I had dinner with Papá's close friends.

During the dinner, I texted my roommate Sarah in Montreal.

I told her that after Papá died, I started to think about death and how it's constantly around us. I started thinking about how I'm eventually going to start losing other people, and I wasn't ready for that.

I didn't know that I would lose Chiara a year later and Nonna Vittoria a year and a half after that.

AFTER THREE SHOTS OF *GRAPPA*, ROCCO DROVE ME AND MOM BACK INTO THE CITY.

Rocco stopped on the one-way street in front of our apartment building. We jolted out, being cautious of the cars coming toward us.

My body ached from the two-hour car ride as we walked towards our apartment building, unlocked the glass door enclosed by metal bars, and stepped into the lobby.

Mom and I waited for the elevator to bring us up to the third floor.

We entered the elevator. It seemed less narrow now with just me and Mom, without Papá and his wheelchair.

The next day, the neighbours in the apartment held a mass for Papá in *Chiesa del* Santissimo Redentore a Val Melaina—the church in front of our apartment. The same church that my great-grandparents attended decades earlier.

MOM AND I ENTERED THE CHURCH, WALKED TOWARDS THE CROSS OF JESUS, AND SAT IN THE PEWS. The blue, orange, and red mural of Jesus at the front of the church began to blur.

chiara

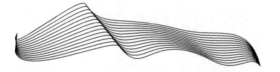

chiara

I WAS TEN YEARS OLD WHEN CHIARA, MY OLDER, AND ONLY SISTER, GOT SICK.

Chiara was five years old when I was born. Mom tells me I always looked up to her. I believe Mom, but I don't have many memories of me and Chiara before she got sick.

I remember Chiara helping me with my third grade home-work, talking me down if I was being too dramatic, or telling me when I was getting my way too much with Mom.

If we got in trouble, Chiara and I would run up the stairs and hide in her room.

We would put our bodies on the door to block Mom from getting in. Chiara blocked the door with the weight of her body, leaning against the door, shoulder first. I would spread my hands out onto the door, thinking I was helping.

I remember Chiara being protective of me.

My memories of Chiara before she got sick are limited because of the trauma that came with Chiara's illness.

I watched Chiara die for ten years. Her body was killing itself.

Her brain was atrophying, but the doctors didn't know why. I didn't understand what was going on. I didn't notice at first.

She was fifteen when she got sick. I was twenty when she died.

When Chiara was dying, I learned now that I experienced two different types of grief.

I experienced ten years of grief when I watched her body shut down. After she died, I experienced the grief of her death. Even though I already felt like I lost Chiara through her illness, it was different when she was no longer physically there.

I experienced coming home to visit Mom, but not seeing Chiara in her hospital bed. I experienced not being able to sit next to her and hold her hand, tell her how my day was, not ever knowing if she heard.

Chiara was in palliative care—an end of life centered care—for ten years at home. She lost her agency—her ability to speak, walk, or function without help.

I watched her body become frail. I watched her have grand mal seizures. I would run to her if I heard her seizing. I would make sure she was safe and hold her. I watched as her bones started to stick out and her face began to sink in.

Chiara went from being able to speak three languages—French, Italian, English—run track, play piano, flute, and guitar, to not being able to speak, walk, or eat without being spoon fed pureed food.

When she was fifteen, she started getting headaches and forgetting how to get home from school.

Mom told me that one time, in the middle of a December night, Chiara climbed out of her bedroom window and onto the roof, barefoot, and in her pyjamas.

She jumped down onto the street to go and look for our dog,

Remy.

The police called Mom and asked if she had a daughter.

Chiara didn't remember her name or address. The police found Mom's contact information in Chiara's phone. They told Mom to meet them at Humber River Hospital.

Remy was inside the whole time.

I slept through it all.

I didn't notice Chiara was getting sick. I would hear Mom and Chiara's boyfriend, Matt, talk about how Chiara was acting differently, but I didn't notice.

When I was in grade eight, Mom arranged that I went to see a counsellor at St. Fidelis Elementary School.

I remember finding a journal the counsellor told me to write in. I wrote that Chiara forgot where the cups went when we put dishes away from the drying rack.

A few months after that, Chiara, Mom, and I were watching TV when Chiara lost control of her bowels. Mom had to help her get cleaned up and changed. After that, her illness progressed quickly.

I noticed then.

When Chiara's illness progressed, Papá moved back in with Mom, Chiara, and me full-time. Nonna Vittoria moved in with us part-time. Everything changed at home.

Mom and Papá would lift Chiara and bring her up the stairs to Mom's bedroom.

During the day, Chiara stayed in a hospital bed in the living room on the main floor.

The living room eventually turned into Chiara's room, with the addition of a queen size bed next to her hospital bed, a commode tucked away in the corner, and Chiara's wheelchair in the middle of the room.

Mom slept with Chiara in this new setup. Papá slept on the couch in the TV room nearby. Nonna slept in Chiara's old room upstairs.

In addition to the new living room setup, strangers kept coming into the house—physiotherapists, occupational therapists, doctors, and nurses.

At night, Sylvia, the night nurse, came three times a week to keep an eye on Chiara's seizures.

Papá would be in the dining room, playing scratch-and-win-tickets, waiting for Sylvia's arrival. Mom and I would watch TV in the TV room nearby.

When the clock on the cable box read 11:00 p.m., I would see Sylvia's headlights from the bay window. I would run up the stairs to my room to avoid small talk. Some nights I stayed.

Mom followed soon after, peeping into my room to say good-night before going to sleep in her own bed.

Papá went to sleep on the caramel leather couch.

In the mornings, we were greeted by Keithsha, the government given personal support worker.

Keithsha watched me grow up. She helped feed and take care of Chiara.

She became family.

Volunteers would occasionally come to help care for Chiara, but

Keithsha, Papá, Mom, and Nonna already had a system in place.

The volunteers would stay with me and help me with homework or drive me to my teenage-centered appointments—eyebrow threading or shopping.

When Papá and Mom would bring Chiara to specialists overseas, I stayed home and Nonna Vittoria looked after me.

In high school, I didn't bring friends over. I was secretive about my home-life. Whenever someone asked if I had any siblings, I would go quiet. I didn't want to delve into the fact that I had an older sister, but she was sick, and even though I'm not an only child it sometimes felt like I was.

It wasn't a feeling I could have explained. I couldn't expect others to understand if I didn't understand myself.

I isolated myself in my room. I spent hours on the computer, watching and editing videos for my projects as a film major at Etobicoke School of the Arts.

I spent most of my childhood escaping, shoving down my emotions, or living in different realities, whether in a good book, video game, blank screen, or good album.

My light brown wooden easel, filled with dried up paint on the edges, stood next to my dresser. My light brown *Seagull* guitar stood on a black stand next to it.

They were also my escape. An escape I brought with me during every move.

I kept myself occupied. I felt like I needed to be strong because Chiara was already sick and Papá and Mom didn't need two sick children.

I self harmed by cutting my wrists in grade eight. I started with razors, then went deeper with knives.

Most of the scars went away except for one on my wrist, which I tried to cover up with my first tattoo when I turned eighteen— an outline of Mykonos for a memorial tattoo of Papá. He visited the island over twenty times.

I soon covered the Mykonos tattoo because it was too painful of a reminder of Papá's loss.

Papá and Mom found out I was cutting, but there wasn't much discussion.

In grade nine, I started cutting in less visible places. Rows of cut skin occupied my upper thighs.

I didn't have conversations with Mom or Papá anymore. They couldn't see the rows.

I stopped after grade nine.

A few days after I found out Papá was dying, I went to my friend's, Roselie's, birthday party. I excused myself, went for a cigarette on her balcony, and put the hot metal part of the lighter on my wrist.

I was sick of being numb. I wanted to feel something in relation to everything I went through.

I knew it was normal to feel, but I didn't feel normal because I wasn't feeling.

AFTER PAPÁ DIED, I MOVED BACK TO TORONTO AND STARTED SCHOOL AT UNIVERSITY OF TORONTO MISSISSAUGA (UTM).

I moved to Oakville, a suburb outside of Mississauga, for my second year at UTM.

Mom called me one night to tell me that Chiara was no longer swallowing her food or able to drink water.

Food is comfort, love, and joy; that is embedded in Italian culture.

Nonna Vittoria loved cooking for her granddaughters. She often made *stracciatella*—a traditional Roman soup that consisted of whipped eggs, homemade chicken broth, a sprinkle of parmesan cheese, and a sprig of parsley.

Nonna Vittoria made this often for Chiara because it was easy to spoon feed her with. Nonna always made extra for me.

Throughout Chiara's illness, Mom pureed Chiara's food so she could spoon feed her.

Having to puree her food didn't stop Mom from only purchasing organic, farm to table, fresh, food. Mom looked for recipes that contained super foods—foods that were good for the body and brain—and spent time preparing and puree-ing them.

She believed that food could act as Chiara's medicine.

Mom told me that not being able to cook for, or feed, Chiara was one of the hardest things to deal with.

This lasted for the final four days of Chiara's life.

AFTER GETTING THE CALL FROM MOM, I CAME BACK TO TORONTO TO ATTEND THE MEETING WITH MOM, AUNT NANCY, UNCLE PAUL, NONNA VITTORIA, AND THE PALLIATIVE CARE TEAM.

The nurse practitioners explained that when the body is in its final stages of shutting down, it loses its ability to swallow.

They said that Mom could no longer feed Chiara or give her water. If she did, Chiara would choke, causing a more painful death than the body shutting itself down.

Mom was instructed to use pink gummy foam-sticks, dip them in water, and put them on Chiara's lips to moisten them if her mouth was dry from not being able to drink.

Two days after the meeting, we moved Chiara to Margaret Bahen Hospice in Newmarket.

AFTER WE GOT CHIARA SETTLED AT THE HOSPICE, I DROVE BACK HOME WITH UNCLE PAUL, NONNA VITTORIA, AND AUNT NANCY. I wanted to stay with Mom and Chiara, but I had a migraine.

I told Mom that I would go home, pack some clothes, and get a good night's sleep so I could spend the remaining days with them in the hospice.

I was hesitant to leave but thought it was for the best.

The next morning, I waited for Uncle Paul, Aunt Nancy, and Nonna Vittoria to pick me up and drive to the hospice.

We planned to go first thing in the morning, but Nancy and Nonna stopped in the cemetery to talk to the director about finding a crypt for Chiara's body.

Before Chiara died, Mom decided that she wanted to cremate Chiara's body. Nonna didn't want her to get cremated because it was against her Roman Catholic beliefs.

AFTER OUR DELAYED JOURNEY, WE FINALLY ARRIVED AT MARGARET BAHEN HOSPICE.

Remy—our dog that Chiara picked out before she got sick—and Nancy's dog, Martén, accompanied us to Chiara's room.

When we arrived, Chiara's hospice room was filled with two of Nonna Vittoria's sisters—my Zias—their three children, Nonna Vittoria, Aunt Nancy, Uncle Paul, Remy, Martén, Mom, and

40

me. I went to give Chiara a kiss, then turned to say hi to everyone.

I turned back from giving kisses to my relatives on their cheeks—the traditional Italian greeting.

Mom came to moisten Chiara's lips with the pink gummy foam-stick. I went to stay with Chiara on the other side of the hospital bed.

Chiara's face looked different.

Her face was sunken in more than usual.

Her eyes looked different. Not glossed over, not a different colour, just vacant.

I knew what this meant.

Mom called the doctor. He confirmed her time of death.

Mom says she left the earth, but where did she go?

It felt like in the exact second I turned away Chiara died. Why did she choose to go then?

It made me question myself.

Did I say hi to Chiara when I arrived, or did I go straight to my relatives?

Why couldn't she wait for me?

Why did I go home last night?

Why did she die? Why was she taken away from me?

Why didn't I have a normal childhood? Why can't I remember the moments that were normal?

Why can't I remember me and Chiara's relationship before the trauma?

I kept yelling "why."

We waited in the hospice room with Chiara's body for eight hours. There was a mix-up with the funeral home. It was a snowy day in November, making the one-hour commute from Toronto to Newmarket longer than usual.

When the funeral directors arrived, they put Chiara's body in a body bag, and placed it on a gurney. The hospice worker laid a multi-coloured, hand sewn quilted blanket on Chiara's body. Paul, the spiritual counsellor, and other staff at the hospice, walked with Mom, Nonna, Uncle Paul, Aunt Nancy, me, and Chiara's body through the hospice and to the black SUV parked outside. We sang *Amazing Grace* as the funeral director rolled Chiara's body down the hall.

I was given ten years and eight hours to grieve my sister's death. It didn't make things easier.

THE FUNERAL HOME'S SUV BROUGHT CHIARA'S BODY TO SICK KIDS HOSPITAL IN TORONTO TO GET AN AUTOPSY, AFTER MOM BEGGED FOR ONE.

For ten years of her life and through her illness, we had no diagnosis.

There was a mention of Creutzfeldt-Jakob disease (CJD) in her medical history, but it was dismissed.

CJD is a disease that can only be confirmed through death.

Because of the mention of CJD in Chiara's record, the autopsy couldn't be done at Sick Kids Hospital. It had to be done in a specialized, controlled environment. Chiara's body was transported to an equipped lab in London, Ontario.

A week later, Chiara's body arrived at the funeral home for cremation and services. Her brain was sent to Ottawa. We had the funeral visitation ceremony a week after Chiara died, and a funeral mass the day after that.

DRESSED IN ALL BLACK, UNCLE PAUL, AUNT NANCY, MOM, NONNA VITTORIA, AND I ARRIVED AT ST. PASCHAL BAYLON'S CHURCH FOR CHIARA'S FUNERAL. I took my thumb, dipped it into the holy water stoup, and traced the sign of the cross over my forehead.

The holy water cooled my sweaty skin.

Woody notes of frankincense engulfed the room as we walked through the mud brown aisle of the church.

The sounds of our footsteps echoed, and the bench in the front row squeaked as we sat and faced the large crucifix, white rose floral arrangements, and Chiara's urn.

SIX MONTHS AFTER CHIARA'S DEATH, MOM WAS CONTACTED BY SICK KIDS HOSPITAL ABOUT THE AUTOPSY RESULTS.

I was in Ottawa visiting my friend, Matt, and had to go back to Toronto early to attend the meeting. I sat at the back row of the train, silently sobbing, coming home from the same city that Chiara's brain was sent to.

When we went to the meeting, the doctors told us that Chiara had Sporadic CJD. They explained that CJD is caused by an abnormal protein in the brain that makes the brain kill itself.

They explained that there are three different types of CJD.

Sporadic meant that there was no understanding of what caused it. Even if we knew about it during her life, there was no cure.

Mom was in shock. We all were. For the ten years of Chiara's illness, there were no answers or diagnosis. Now that we had a diagnosis, there were still no answers.

Chiara's was a rare case, as the average life expectancy of someone with Sporadic CJD is less than twelve months.

CJD is unheard of for people her age.

The doctors at Sick Kids Hospital asked Mom if they could write a paper on Chiara's case because it was so rare.

MY EYES GLAZED OVER AS I READ ABOUT CHIARA IN THE *OXFORD JOUR-NAL OF NEUROPATHOLOGY & EXPERIMENTAL NEUROLOGY*.

Chiara—and my family's—journey was laid in cold, clinical scientific terms, but it still didn't make sense to me.

nonna

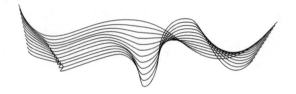

nonna

I WAS TWENTY-ONE YEARS OLD WHEN NONNA VITTORIA WAS DIAG-
NOSED WITH STAGE FOUR METASTASIZED CANCER.

Mom, Aunt Nancy, Nonna, and I were on vacation in Naples,
Florida.

Classes at UTM were on hold for Christmas Break.

Nonna wasn't feeling well on the trip. Her body itched and she
didn't have much of an appetite. She barely ate or wanted to eat.

Nonna Vittoria looked weak.

The skin on her face was thinner. Even though she sunbathed
her already deep-olive-skin, it still somehow managed to look
pale. Her skin was sweaty, but not from the sun or the heat.

One night, I was sitting next to Nonna on the couch. She dozed
off while we watched TV.

This was normal for Nonna. She would often doze off when we
watched shows in English, or if she was tired while we watched
Tempesta D'amore, the German-dubbed-Italian soap opera.

But this was a different type of dozing off.

She sunk a little more than usual on the couch. Her face
showed grimace. Her face was clammy. Her body was thinner. I
thought she looked like Papá when we went to visit him in Rome
for the last month of his life, but I dismissed the feeling.

WE CUT OUR VACATION SHORT AND RESCHEDULED OUR FLIGHT BACK TO TORONTO TO AN EARLIER DATE.

Nonna Vittoria wasn't feeling any better. She hadn't gone to the bathroom in a week, and her stomach pain was getting worse.

When we got back to Toronto, Uncle Paul drove Mom, Nonna Vittoria, and Aunt Nancy to Sunnybrook Hospital.

I stayed home to unpack from Florida and get ready for my trip to New York to visit my friend, and old roommate, Leah.

Leah and I lived together in our apartment in Oakville. When Chiara died, I moved back in with Mom. After the lease was up, Leah moved to New York.

I had a feeling that I should've gone to the hospital with Aunt Nancy, Mom, and Nonna Vittoria, but I ignored it.

Mom called me during the hospital visit to update me. She told me that Nonna was waiting for a Computed Tomography (CT) scan.

When I hung up the phone, I googled why a CT scan was needed for stomach pain.

The results showed cancer.

I paced back and forth and kept looking at the search results on my phone, anxiously waiting for another update. I tensed and untensed my legs to a rhythm. I looked at *WebMD* on my laptop and *Healthline* on my phone.

Mom called me a few hours later and confirmed what I thought I already knew.

The doctors didn't know where it started or how long it was

there, but there was cancer in Nonna Vittoria's liver and lungs, and it was spreading. They sent in a referral for Nonna to see an oncologist at Humber River Hospital.

After the appointment at Sunnybrook Hospital, Uncle Paul drove Mom back home with Nonna Vittoria in the passenger seat. I went out to the car, gave Nonna a hug, and sat in the backseat.

"*Ti voglio bene,*" I said to her. *I love you.*

I cancelled my trip to New York the next morning.

NONNA VITTORIA AND I HAD A CLOSE RELATIONSHIP.

Though the English to Italian translation made it difficult for her to understand what I went to school for—since it was neither Law nor Medicine—she loved me fiercely.

Nonna had her own house on Keelegate Drive and lived with Uncle Paul. When Chiara got sick, she went back and forth between her home and ours. She stayed with me, Chiara, Papá, and Mom on our house on Burr Avenue most often.

I grew up with her.

I remember coming home from St. Fidelis Elementary School to Nonna's deliciously cooked steak or pasta, with fresh handmade noodles and sauce made from the tomatoes in her garden.

I remember coming home to a clean room, unable to find the things I left scattered on the floor. I remember being angry that I couldn't find things.

I missed that feeling when I moved out.

UNCLE PAUL, AUNT NANCY, MOM, AND I BROUGHT NONNA VITTORIA TO THE ONCOLOGIST APPOINTMENT AT HUMBER RIVER HOSPITAL.

Nonna immigrated from Italy to Toronto in 1955. She was twenty years old.

She learned English herself but didn't understand it fully. Mom and I would often bring Nonna to appointments with her doctors and help translate the results.

The oncologist confirmed what the doctors told us at Sunnybrook.

Nonna Vittoria had cancer and it was terminal. It was spreading quickly. I asked the doctor for a timeline.

She told me Nonna Vittoria had six months left to live.

In a panic, Aunt Nancy translated the news to Nonna after the appointment.

Nonna said she wished she hadn't known.

A few days after receiving the news, Mom, Aunt Nancy, and I moved in with Uncle Paul and Nonna Vittoria on Keelegate Drive. I wanted to stay present with her and cherish the time we had left together.

I had to go back to UTM in January, but I dropped a few courses so I could spend more time at home with Nonna.

When summer came, I needed to take summer courses to catch up with the ones that I dropped during the winter term.

During that time, Nonna grew weaker and was sleeping more. Even though she slept for most of the day, I felt guilty leaving her.

I missed the first few classes and read my *Social Media and Electronic Commerce Law* textbook next to Nonna as she slept.

NONNA WAS A DEVOUT ROMAN CATHOLIC.

When she was dying of cancer, Father Gigi of St. Norbert's Church came over to her house three times.

She would talk to him in English through her thick Italian accent, and he would talk to her in Italian with his English accent.

She talked to him for the first two visits but wasn't able to on his third.

The ladies from St. Norbert's Church came on the last Sunday of every month to give Nonna communion and pray. They visited six times for the six months of her illness.

I DON'T REMEMBER THE EXACT MOMENT I FELL OUT OF RELIGION.

I don't think there was one.

It was just about being told something has to be a certain way your whole life, and then realizing it doesn't have to be. It was about being away from the monthly church visits at St. Fidelis Elementary School—away from the structured and predetermined milestones; Communion, Confirmation, Ash Wednesday.

When I went to Etobicoke School of the Arts, I heard about other perspectives, religions, and viewpoints. I realized that Catholicism didn't align with my own.

Before Papá's funeral, I hadn't stepped into a church since I received my confirmation five years prior.

When Nonna Vittoria got sick, I rediscovered a comfort in the act of praying. Zia Mimmina and Zia Vincenza—her sisters—Mom, Aunt Nancy, Uncle Paul, and I said the rosary with Nonna. When she was unable to speak or open her eyes on the last few days of her life, I read prayers to her.

Though I didn't reconcile with my Catholicism, I found comfort in these prayers and saw them more as poetry.

In the last few days of Nonna's illness, when she was no longer able to talk, her sisters encouraged me to read prayers to her.

I would grab the prayer cards that were housed on Nonna's polished oak dresser, sit next to Nonna, and read them to her.

The paper prayer cards with photos of *San* Rocco—the patron saint of Nonna's hometown Collelongo—*Sant'*Antonio, and Jesus were tucked away in the mirror. On the dresser, wooden prayer cards stood tall. Voices of different tones and ages reading Italian prayers came from the radio next to Nonna's bed every night and every morning.

Two days before Nonna died, Zia Mimmina, Zia Vincenza, Mom, Aunt Nancy, Uncle Paul, and I sat around Nonna and followed along the rosary that blared out from the radio. The day before she died, I found her green prayer book and prayed to her.

In the last hours of Nonna's life, Mom, Aunt Nancy, Uncle Paul, and I sat around Nonna praying and chanting *Ave Maria*.

NONNA VITTORIA DIED AT HOME.

We asked the funeral home for extra time with her body.

Zia Mimmina, Zia Vincenza, and Nonna's neighbours came over to sit with her body in her bedroom.

She died around noon. The funeral directors picked her body up at four. Her visitation was two days later, and the mass was the day after that.

I felt a lot more anger with Nonna's death. An anger I didn't feel before. Why did she have to die so quickly after Chiara did? Why did she have to die, too?

The night Nonna died, Danub, my friend since third grade, brought me a bottle of *Sauza* tequila and margarita mix. We sat on the bleachers at Maple Leaf Park, a park down the street from St. Fidelis Elementary School.

We made overflowing drinks in small plastic cups. We discussed whether or not the Bible was a book of poetry that people took too literally. We discussed existence, death, and climate change.

I yelled at the sky and told him how pissed off I was that everyone around me had to die.

MOM, AUNT NANCY, UNCLE PAUL, AND I ARRIVED AT ST. NORBERT'S CHURCH FOR NONNA VITTORIA'S FUNERAL.

The funeral director hoisted Nonna's wooden maple casket with bronze figures of The Last Supper and laid it on top of a black foldable rack.

The pallbearers, my second-cousins—Carmen, Christopher, Frank, Daniel, Carlo, and John—walked towards the casket, put on their white gloves, and got into position. They grasped the handles of the casket and lifted Nonna off the nylon straps of the rack.

I unzipped my bag and grabbed the white rose petals that the funeral director handed out before shutting the casket. I grabbed an extra handful for the church.

The pallbearers brought Nonna's casket up the cement stairs. I sprinkled the rose petals behind her path into the church.

The funeral singer's voice echoed the lyrics of *Ave Maria* while the organ echoed the melody.

The pallbearers carried Nonna's casket into the smoke-filled, sweet palo-santo-scented church.

canada day

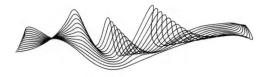

canada day

IT WAS IMPORTANT TO ME THAT I WAS THERE WHEN NONNA VITTORIA DIED.

I had a lot of guilt for not being mentally present when Papá died. I was angry that I wasn't given enough time to be.

I was going to deal with Nonna's death differently. I was going to spend as much time as I could with her—ask her questions about her life and give her updates on mine.

When I look back at the times nearing Nonna's death and where I was, I think about my state of anxiety every time I left the house.

I think about my friend Roselie's graduation—three weeks before Nonna Vittoria passed—checking my phone constantly for an update on something going wrong during the ceremony.

I remember celebrating Canada Day when Nonna was at the phase of dying where she slept all day.

NONNA LAYS DOWN ON HER QUEEN SIZE ORGANIC COTTON MATTRESS THAT WE BOUGHT HER WHEN SHE WAS DIAGNOSED WITH CANCER.

We knew she would be spending a lot of time in bed, and Nonna hadn't changed her mattress since before Nonno Carlo died, fourteen years earlier.

Nonna told me that there was an Italian man with a big white truck that drove on their street selling mattresses. Some of her neighbours had already bought one from him. Nonna and Nonno decided to do the same.

The mattress had grown stiff and worn over the years.

I walk to the other side of Nonna's bed, plop myself next to her, and turn my body to face her.

The occupational therapist that showed me, Mom, Aunt Nancy, and Uncle Paul how to safely and properly lift Nonna out from her bed had just left. She mentioned getting a hospital bed for Nonna because it would be easier for the progression of her illness. Nonna was growing weaker every day and wasn't able to give enough force to help us get her out of bed.

Nonna got defensive at the mention of a hospital bed. She didn't want to give up her bed set. It was a wedding present she received when Nonno Carlo and her got married in 1955.

Despite being over sixty years old, the bronzed frame still shined, and the brass lamps on the nightstands were never replaced. Rosaries, Chiara's funeral card, and two Golden Pear Soaps were housed together in her nightstand drawer.

I bought Nonna Vittoria Golden Pear Soap for Christmas when I worked for Lush Cosmetics. It was a sparkly golden soap, shaped like a pear, with a strong sweet pear scent.

Nonna would always make *pere cotte*, boiled pears, for me and Chiara to eat. The boiled pears were easy to spoon feed Chiara with, and I loved the robust cinnamon scent that would come out of the kitchen when she cooked them. Nonna loved the scent of the soap.

My co-workers put four on hold for me on my next shift, so I could buy more for Nonna. They were a seasonal product, and I wanted to stock up for her.

Two years after I bought them, Nonna still hadn't used them. She left them scattered through her drawers and house for the *profumo*.

"*Nonna, forse ti sentiresti più comoda in un letto d'ospedale*," I say to her, explaining that she might be more comfortable in a hospital bed.

It was going to get more difficult for her to get out of bed for wheelchair transfers, or to sit up to eat, though the prescribed steroids eventually stopped working, and she lost her appetite again, making this no longer a concern.

She would soon become completely bedridden.

"*Forse hai ragione*," she replies.

Hearing her say *maybe you're right* was the first time in the weeks of conversations about getting a hospital bed where she agreed or thought about it more before shutting the idea out completely.

She trusted me.

NONNA SLEEPS ON THE RENTED RESPITE HOSPITAL BED THAT WAS DE-LIVERED A FEW WEEKS PRIOR. Her bronze-framed queen size bed remains next to the hospital bed. I sit on her old bed, next to her, reading a book, watching her sleep from the corner of my eye, and waiting for her to wake up so I could spend some time with her. Most days were like this.

Bzz

I check my vibrating phone and see a message from my friend Max pop up.

Is anyone free today? he asks the group chat consisting of me, Annmarie, and Manon. Max lives in Sweden for school and is visiting for the summer.

I look at Nonna sleeping, look down on my phone, and look at the self-created rash on my arm—a habit I picked up over the years from nervously scratching. *Maybe it's a good idea to get out of the house.*

I get off Nonna's bed and go to the front room kitchen where Mom sits at the table.

"Max invited me to his dad's house for Canada Day," I tell her.

"You should go," she replies.

"Are you sure it's okay if I do?" I ask Mom.

"Yes," she replies.

"Okay. But text me if Nonna wakes up," I say. "I'll come right back."

I WAS IN THAT STRETCH OF TIME THAT DETERMINES IF YOU'RE TOO LATE TO CANCEL ON SOMEONE WHEN MAX TEXTED ME THAT HE WAS TEN MINUTES AWAY.

I run to the basement, enter the laundry room, and rustle through the rack of hanging clothes. I find a black one-piece bathing suit. I sprint back up the stairs, bathing suit in hand, and go to the bathroom.

I place my phone on the porcelain countertop, open the medicine cabinet, and search for my pink *Bic* razor through orange prescription bottles. I pull down my romper, close the toilet seat and put my leg up on the seat.

I glide the razor on my dry skin. Skin particles and hair follicles fall off my ashy skin.

My phone vibrates on the sink, and Max's name lights up on the screen.

"We'll be there in five," he says in an amplified, muffled voice.

I hang up the phone, continue shaving, and nick myself. Blood pools on my leg. I grab a paper towel, press it on my skin and watch the white paper soak a bright red hue.

I change into my bathing suit and put my romper back on.

I tiptoe into Nonna's room and check on her. She's still sleeping. I blow her a kiss from the door frame and exit her room.

I grab a towel from the linen closet, put it in my bag, and walk towards the door.

"Love you," I say to Mom.

"Text me if she wakes up," I say.

I STEP OUTSIDE ON THE FRONT PORCH AND LIGHT A CIGARETTE.

The mixture of humidity and smoke weigh down my lungs. Max drives his Mom's 2018 white Honda CRV onto Nonna's street. I go down the porch steps and walk towards the car.

"Sorry, just lit this," I say to Max.

"How are you *bella*?" he asks.

I shrug my shoulders and take a drag from my cigarette.

I throw my cigarette on the ground, stomp on it, walk to the other side of the car and get in.

Max puts his sunroof down and we make our way to his dad's apartment.

BZZ

My phone vibrates on my lap.

Plates filled with pasta and tomato sauce, and glasses filled with red wine, cover the round table in Max's dad's apartment. I look at the screen of my phone.

Nonna's awake now.

I close the text from Mom, look up at the plates filled with food, see Max's dad grating parmesan cheese by the stove, and type a text back.

How is she? Is she okay? I'll be there soon.

I place my phone back onto my lap and twirl spaghetti on my fork.

Bzz

I eat my spaghetti, take a sip of wine, engage in small talk, and bounce my leg under the table.

I ARRIVE AT KEELEGATE DRIVE.

I walk into Nonna's room and sit on one of the four empty chairs next to her bed.

She lies there asleep. I sit there for a while, watching her. I go back to the living room and see Mom, Aunt Nancy, and Uncle Paul.

"I'm sorry I missed it. Did you tell her I was gone?" I ask Mom.

"Yeah," Mom responds. "She asked about you."

A couple of hours go by and Nonna wakes up. I go into her room and sit next to her on her bed.

"Hi Nonna." I give her a kiss on the cheek.

"*Dove eri?*" she asks, her voice shaky and weak.

I reply to her question. "I went to see some friends."

"*Hai fatto bene,*" she says, smiling.

I didn't feel that way though. Maybe I did the right thing for my mind by getting out of the house, but it didn't feel like the right thing missing one of the few moments I had left with her.

Eleven days later, Nonna Vittoria never woke up again.

window of tolerance

window of tolerance

WE CUT OUR TRIP SHORT.

Max, Matt, Manon, and I drove to Stratford, Ontario to spend the last weekend in August together before going back to our lives in September—Max back to Sweden, Matt back to Ottawa, Manon back to work, and me back to my final year at UTM.

The August heat slows us down as we walk towards Nathalie's, Max's Mom's, white Honda CRV.

Max is driving us back to Toronto for the one-month mass of Nonna Vittoria's death.

THE HAPPENING OF, WHAT I CALL, A DEATH-IVERSARY IS ONE THAT AL-WAYS MAKES ME EVALUATE THE PASSING OF TIME.

For Papá's one-month-death-iversary, time went by fast, but felt slow.

Papá died a month after we were told his cancer came back. I moved from Montreal to Toronto, Toronto to Rome, and Rome to Toronto in the matter of two months.

The time marker of what a month was, during what I went through with Papá, was one that was so skewed that it made time feel stuck.

The days leading up to Papá's one-month-mass felt like a plane landing—my stomach in a pit, the descent quite grand, but only minutes to get there.

When his death-iversary happened, time felt still again. My grief was on standby, waiting for a safe moment to accompany me on the descending flight of grieving.

I wish I had been able to spend more time with Papá prior to his last month of life.

I was in Montreal before he got sick. I didn't get to spend the last few months of his life with him when he was healthy.

Even though I was with him physically during his cancer, it didn't feel like I was.

That was when my dissociative episodes were at their peak. I was living in a depersonalized state. I felt outside of my body.

I felt like I aged ten years from the time between Chiara's death and her one-year-death-iversary. Not because time went slow, but because that's how it felt.

I was tired. I was burnt out. I dropped out of classes in school, tried to make them up, and isolated myself.

The year after Chiara's death, I was living in a state of anxiety. In fight or flight mode.

This started almost instantly after her death.

A few moments after she died, I went outside to get fresh air. I got a phone call from an unknown number and answered it like my sister didn't just die a few minutes earlier.

I finished writing an essay on the night of her funeral for my *Communication Research Methods* class. Even though I had petitioned for an extension on my essay, it hadn't been approved yet and I convinced myself I needed to have my essay done by the due date just in case.

I don't remember a lot about the year after Chiara passed.

During Papá's one-month-mass, I felt like it was a year since he passed. For Chiara's one-year-mass, it felt like a month.

It was impossible for me to believe that a full year went by.

When Chiara died, I tried to go see a trauma counsellor. I went for two sessions and started to ignore her emails when she tried to make another appointment. There was one thing that she told me that stuck out, though.

Window of Tolerance.

Traumatic events decrease your window of tolerance, making it smaller, and making most of your time in either a hypo-aroused—meaning a depressed or slow—state, or a hyper-aroused—meaning an anxious or flighty—state.

When in a hypo-aroused state, memory issues and dissociation may occur, and it did for me. You can often feel outside of your body. I did.

It's why I can't remember a lot of my childhood.

I was ten years old and too young to understand what was going on when Chiara got sick. I can't remember memories of her because I kept tiptoeing between a hyper and hypo aroused state. I was tiptoeing between manic and depressed.

My window of tolerance was already shrinking during Chiara's illness.

When Papá and Chiara died, it felt like it closed shut.

Nonna's death was different from Papá and Chiara's. The four weeks leading up to the one-month-death-iversary mass felt long.

It felt like the whole flight.

It was the most recent of the three deaths—Papá was first and Chiara was second—but it was the first time that I was there for it all. I was there when Nonna was diagnosed with Stage Four metastasized cancer. I moved in with her when she was sick. I was there when she died.

I was trying to open up my window of tolerance again, allowing little rays of light to come through, so I could enjoy the last few moments we had together and not feel the same guilt I felt with Papá.

WE ARRIVE IN TORONTO AND DRIVE PAST THE MAIN ENTRANCE OF ST. NORBERT'S CHURCH. Max pulls Nathalie's white CRV into the parking lot, parks the car, and turns back to me. I let out a breath, grip the handle of the car door, and exit the Honda.

Aunt Nancy smokes a cigarette in front of the grey, grand steps.

I walk past her, plant my feet on the steps, grab the black rail, and haul myself up the next step. My eyes glance over at the peaking pink, red, and white botanicals that reside next to the railing.

The two large doors of the church, held open by strings, reveal a crowd of people waiting in the foyer.

I squirm past the crowd and into the frankincense scented chambers of the church. I dip my hand in the tepid Holy Water enclosed by a golden bowl, bow to Jesus, and sign the cross on my forehead. I look for Mom in the pews. The mass begins.

mashed potatoes, pumpkin pie and grief

mashed potatoes, pumpkin pie and grief

MOM, REMY, AND I DRIVE BY ST. NORBERT'S CHURCH ON OUR WAY TO NONNA'S VITTORIA'S HOUSE ON KEELEGATE DRIVE.

Mom parks Nonno Carlo's hand-me-down 1997 Honda CRV in the driveway where he had his heart attack fourteen years prior.

Remy was just a puppy then.

Nonno put Remy on a leash out front when he loaded up the car to go pick Nonna up from Mom's house.

Nonno's heart stopped when he was loading the car. Remy frantically barked when Nonno collapsed on the floor. The front neighbour called 911.

Remy continued to bark when the paramedics arrived.

I WAS EIGHT YEARS OLD THE DAY NONNO CARLO DIED.

I waited for Mom in the Kiss and Ride outside St. Fidelis Elementary School. Cars passed, but Mom's didn't.

Our neighbours, Robert and Steven's dad, Carlo, came to pick me up and bring me to their house. Steven was in the same class as Chiara before she transferred to De La Salle College Oaklands.

Mom picked me up from their house later that night.

When Mom broke the news to me and Chiara, I choked on

the kernels from the bag of microwaved popcorn I was given to snack on at Robert and Steven's house.

Now, fourteen years later, it's our thirteenth Thanksgiving without Nonno Carlo, third without Papá, second without Chiara, and first without Nonna Vittoria.

MOM GETS REMY OUT OF THE BACK SEAT OF THE CAR, HIS FUR GREY AND TEETH DECAYING.

The Ultimate Oldies radio station blares through the open garage door. The door that goes into the backyard from the garage is held open by a string.

Mom, Remy, and I walk through the garage, passing old wheelchairs, walkers, and commodes.

Remy tugs Mom through the door of the backyard and towards Uncle Paul. Uncle Paul takes the weeds out of Nonna's now wilted garden.

I take out the string that holds the door open from its latch and shut the door. Mom takes Remy off his leash. He wanders into the backyard, sniffing the grass, trees, and Nonna Vittoria's garden. Nonna was too sick to plant her garden this year, so Mom did.

Mom walks over to the other side of the garden and picks the wild tomatoes—tomatoes she didn't plant, but ones that still sprouted bountiful and sweet from Nonna's garden last year.

I sit on the patio steps and stare at the fence that divides the neighbouring backyard with Nonna's backyard. I stare at the foilage covered patch of dirt on our side of the fence.

"Plants are growing on top of Annabelle," I say to Uncle Paul.

"Yeah, more weeds," he responds.

ANNABELLE WAS MY CAT FOR SEVEN YEARS.

She was the runt of the litter and looked like a kitten even when she grew up.

When Papá was alive, Annabelle would always place her black, white, and orange body on top of his scratch-and-win lottery tickets while he was playing.

When Nonna got diagnosed with cancer, we brought Annabelle and Remy with us on our move to Keelegate Drive.

Annabelle was an indoor/outdoor cat. If she stayed out all night, she would *meow* at the patio door that was in front of the futon I was sleeping on in Nonna's TV room.

Annabelle didn't come in one morning.

When she didn't come in the second morning, I thought that maybe she had gone back to Mom's house on Patricia Avenue.

When she didn't come in the third morning, my friend Roselie and I put up posters around the neighbourhood, covering them with clear-packing-tape to protect them from the rain that was expected that night.

When she didn't come home for four days, I got a call minutes after clocking in for my shift working the front desk at Ink and Water Tattoo.

I put the customer on the work phone on hold and saw my phone buzzing on the desk with the same number that called me three times, minutes before.

"I think I saw your cat dead in the front of my driveway," she said.

I STARE AT THE WEEDS GROWING ON TOP OF ANNABELLE'S GRAVE FOR
ANOTHER MOMENT AND GET UP FROM THE PATIO STEPS.

"I'm going to go in and start cooking," I yell to Mom and Uncle Paul.

I exit through the garage and enter Nonna's house through the side door.

I go to the basement and sit down at the kitchen table. Mom enters through the side door moments after. She walks past me and into the *cantina*.

She exits the *cantina* with a sack of potatoes and brings them to the sink. I push my chair out and walk towards Mom.

I hear a car coming into the driveway. I peep out of the kitchen window and see Aunt Nancy's white Fiat 500. I walk back into the kitchen and towards the sink. Mom grabs two knives from the drawer and hands one to me. We peel the potatoes and start preparing Thanksgiving lunch.

annabelle

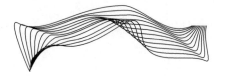

annabelle

ANNABELLE WAS MY CAT FOR SEVEN YEARS.

Thea, an acquaintance at St. Fidelis Elementary School, had a cat who gave birth to a litter.

After seeing Thea's announcement on *BlackBerry Messenger*, I eagerly ran down the stairs from my bedroom and petitioned to Mom and Papá. They said no.

"It's too much work," said Mom.

"I don't want to be taking care of a cat, too," she said.

With all the new people coming in and out of our home, and the decline in Chiara's health, our house on Burr Avenue got hectic quickly.

WHEN CHIARA WAS THIRTEEN YEARS OLD, SHE LOOKED UP DIFFERENT BREEDS OF DOGS AND FOUND A COTON DE TULEAR BREEDER IN MONTREAL.

"I found a dog!" Chiara said to Mom, with a printed photo of a white and brown fluffy dog with deep brown eyes. Coton De Tulears get their name from looking like puffs of cotton.

After some pleading, Chiara convinced Mom to let us get Remy.

Chiara set everything up, and all we needed to do next was get Remy to Toronto from Montreal.

We went to pick Remy up at Pearson airport and brought him to our house on Burr Avenue.

Before Chiara got sick, she would take Remy for walks, feed him, and take care of him. He would sleep on her bed and follow her around.

When Chiara got sick, Mom had to take care of Remy, Chiara, and me.

AFTER DAYS OF PLEADING, I FINALLY CONVINCED PAPÁ AND MOM TO LET ME ADD ANOTHER ADDITION TO OUR FAMILY: THE RUNT OF THE LITTER CALICO WHO LOOKED LIKE TROUBLE.

We went to pick up Annabelle from Thea's house.

On Annabelle's first night at Burr Avenue, she slept with me under the covers, softly *meowing* and waking me up every couple of hours.

When Annabelle was a kitten, she was tiny enough to fit in the openings of our shoes and sneak in the space below the fridge.

Annabelle was a spunky cat who jumped on counters, *meowed* in conversations, and ran every time she heard the crinkle of the treat bag.

She sat on Mom's chest when Mom cried. She circled our feet when we put our shoes on. She slept with me almost every night.

She changed the entire atmosphere of Burr Avenue.

I WAS SURPRISED THAT I ALLOWED MYSELF TO GRIEVE ANNABELLE SO VISCERALLY.

My whole body shook. My breathing was heavy.

I violently sobbed in Mom's car when she picked me up from

work after I received the news.

I didn't just lose a cat; I lost my support system. I lost my sleep-aid. I lost the little *meows* in protest to stop me and Mom from yelling at each other and just stop to laugh at Annabelle.

Annabelle made everything just bearable.

When I lost Annabelle, all my trauma came to the surface. She was no longer there to help me shove it down or make it tolerable.

We knew Nonna Vittoria was going to die in a few months. Did I have to lose the being that would help me through it all, too?

Remy was still around, and though I loved him dearly, he was always Chiara's. Annabelle was mine.

Her death added to a never-ending list of losses; her memory added a ray of light to a traumatic past.

holy rosary

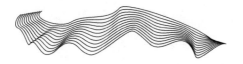

holy rosary

"MARRIAGE IS A PROMISE BETWEEN MAN, WIFE, AND GOD."

The priest stands in the front chambers of Holy Rosary Parish, in Toronto, wearing a white vestment. His voice echoes through the large confines of the church.

It's my first time in this church, and the first time in eight years that I attend a mass that's not a funeral or a death milestone.

My second cousin Alessandra stands at the front chambers of the church near the priest. Her white lace wedding gown flows over her body, and her face is painted with pink-blushed cheeks and lightly lined eyes. Michael, her fiancé—in minutes, husband—stands beside her in a black suit and teal tie. I haven't met Michael before today.

I bounce my leg and thank God that the pews are drilled to the ground and don't shake as my leg does.

My mind wanders as the priest rambles about how the wife is meant to carry her husband's children, promising to raise them in the Catholic church.

I try to focus on the loving glance that my cousin and her soon to be husband exchange, but my eyes wander to the stained-glass window of Jesus carrying the cross behind them.

The priest speaks about how suffering is a crucial part of Catholicism.

I ALWAYS WONDERED IF I WERE TO GET MARRIED, WOULD I GET MAR-
RIED IN A CHURCH?

There's a church on Dufferin and St. Clair with large concrete
steps, that I always thought would be a perfect place to take a
picture in my wedding dress—fitted long lace sleeves with a puffy
ballroom skirt. The long train would drape over the steps, and I
would have one hand on my hip.

"Can you still get married in a church if you're not religious?" I
ask Mom.

"Sure. Nancy got married at a nondenominational church,"
she replies.

Aunt Nancy and her ex-husband, Phil, divorced the year I was
born. I always tease that I was the ray of sunshine in a rather
dark year of her life. She agrees.

Growing up Roman Catholic, churches were the only place I
knew when it came to marriage. Growing up, I didn't see anyone
get married anywhere else.

When I realized I might not marry a man, the idea of get-
ting married at a church seemed daunting. When I realized I
might not be Catholic, the idea seemed fleeting. When I realized
I might not get married at all, the idea seemed to matter less.

No matter how fleeting the idea was, or how probable me get-
ting married was, it was nice to think of the traditional implica-
tions that getting married at a church entailed.

Papá died, so he couldn't walk me down the aisle. When Chi-
ara got sick, I knew from a young age that she wouldn't be able
to be my maid of honour.

I couldn't have those traditions, so the tradition of getting married at a church seemed nice.

AS THE PRIEST RAVES ON ABOUT HOW SUFFERING IS AN INTEGRAL PART OF CATHOLICISM, I WONDER IF WHAT I'VE EXPERIENCED COUNTS?

I suffered watching my sister get sick. I suffered when I saw her body kill itself, her brain slowly attacking itself.

She suffered from nightmares, headaches, seizures, confusion, and ultimately incapacitation.

Papá suffered when he turned to alcohol to cope with watching his daughter become debilitatingly ill.

He suffered when he was given pills to control his cancer, only for it to come back worse.

Only for us to have one month with him before he died.

Only for me to suffer from the guilt of not having a better relationship with him when he was alive.

Mom suffered from trying everything but not being able to save her daughter. She watched her daughter die for ten years.

She suffered from watching her relationship with her husband crumble under the stress of the new, medical, turmoil-ridden environment—able to withstand the long-distance but not a dying daughter.

Nonna Vittoria suffered when she had stomach pain, only to go to the hospital to find out she had cancer.

My family suffered when we lost not one, not two, but three people in our family in the span of three years.

I suffered by getting further away from the person I was before grief. Before I watched everyone around me die.

I suffered by shoving down my grief and feeling isolated because my grieving didn't look like other people's.

I suffered when my grief demanded to be felt and shoving it down didn't work anymore.

No matter how tired my hands were from shoving, I kept on trying.

THE LOW-HANGING LIGHTS CREATE A GLOW ON THE BRIDE AND GROOM. The organs blare and the crowd cheers as the newly-wed couple walk down the narrow path between the two rows of pews.

"I don't think I want to get married in a church anymore," I turn and say to Mom.

She smiles.

"Honey, I'll support you no matter what."

POETRY

bones

red soil occupies my flesh,
your bones

I'll lay here until I'm dead
I'll lay here until my skin stains red
until the soil turns to mud and the slippery tracks lead to
you and

your bones
engulfed by sticky mud

your bones
placed in a wooden box

your bones
red seas of memories

your bones
lay at rest

but I will not rest until

your bones
escape their boundings

until
the mud dries up

until
my red stained skin settles
until
yours, no longer pale

pull out the dirt
your bones
cannot rest while I'm still yelling

I'll keep throwing dirt
until
your bones are
no longer covered

your bones
have lost feeling
my God,

your bones decay
while mine

sara margherita

try healing

heaven

There's a flickering light on the cemetery wall,
I wonder if someone got lost on their way to their resting place?

A hole on the wall,
A place in the ground

Some even argue,
All around

the quiet room

We find comfort in nooks of hospice rooms,
People no longer fighting for their lives

Doors painted the same colour grey as
Hospital rooms

Clinics filled with cold air
Dense coughs

Hold tightly the hand of my mother,
This sight too familiar to see

This frayed string that ties us together

Hums of foreign machines carry
From room to room

Fake plants hang from walls
Not able to give oxygen

Pale light emits from the ceiling,

waves

Emits the remnants of my father,
My sister,
Your brother

Voices of machines blare loudly
While vocal cords
Too weak

Yellowing skin turns pale

We all live differently but die the same

morphine

I wonder if you can feel the different kisses
With your eyes closed,
Morphine in

I wonder if you know whose lips belong to who
When I say I love you,
I wonder if you hear?

grief looks like

Grief became embedded in my existence.
When my dad died, I didn't get out of bed for three days.
My grief looked like that.

My grief looked like a chameleon, shaping its appearance
depending on the surrounding I was in.

My grief looked like its favourite game was hide and seek.

My grief looked like having one too many drinks at my cousin's
wedding. I saw her sister commence a toast and realized I didn't
have a sister to do that for me anymore.

Grief looks like three.

Three drinks in my system when my heart starts racing and the
blood pumps to my face when I see the father-daughter dance.

I count to ten until the song slows down

I stare at the ceiling

Grab my clutch and my lipstick
The same shade as my face

Grief looks like
Sunburnt peeling skin
Pinching colour in your cheeks

Like broken collar bones
Stay still

Grief looks like
Crushed rose petals and metal wire

Rose-coloured glasses
With a darker hue

Black ink sprawled out on a
Crossed out word

Grief looks like
"Are you an only child?"
"I had a sister, but she died"

Grief looks like
"What do your parents do for a living?"
Cancer didn't give him that choice

Grief looks like
An invisibility cloak
Blistering fingers and
Picked skin off of nails

Grief looks like

A prank gone too far
A lottery you didn't want to win

Grief looks like
A chameleon playing hide and seek
Until it's ready to be found

home for the holidays

The day I was told my dad was dying,
I cried for two hours then went on with my day
Like nothing happened

life

I feel most alive when my heart is still beating
Veins have heat in
Lungs,
Stale breathing

twenty twenty

thought there would be a transformation when 2020 arrived

a surge going through me,
a new decade
a new energy

I was a little less sad this New Year's Eve
surrounded by love, bubbles, red wine, and
Staining teeth

I was a little less sad this New Year's Eve
surrounded by friends
Alive
not dying

I was a little less sad this New Year's Eve
until I woke up
it was 2020

And I wasn't a little less sad

birthday

Staring drunk in the mirror
Everything comes up
Trying to have fun

Dancing works for some people

Maybe it's just a moment in the haze
And then I'm okay

Everything is situational
And in this situation, I'm mostly okay
But there are moments I'm not

My friend tells me her dead mom came to see her in a dream
She said she mentioned me

Told her to keep me close

jade

I wonder if the rays of sunshine help
Or if flowers just rot in the soil they get buried in?

epilogue

AS I FINISHED MY FINAL EDITS OF THIS BOOK, I RECEIVED NEWS THAT NONNA RINA HAD A HEART ANEURYSM AND DIED THE NEXT DAY.

I couldn't publish this book without acknowledging the loss of Nonna Rina.

Four months before Nonna Rina passed, Mom and I went to Rome to visit her, see the Colosseum, and eat *supplì* from the hot table near our apartment. After Papà and Chiara died, Mom and I would try to go to Rome at least once a year to visit Nonna Rina and other family members. We weren't able to that year because of Nonna Vittoria's cancer diagnosis and death in Toronto.

Before our most recent trip, it had been a year and a half since Mom and I visited Rome and Nonna Rina.

"I DON'T WANT IT TO BE A FULL TWO YEARS BEFORE SEEING NONNA RINA."

I told Mom, on the phone, on my bus ride back home from school. My *History and Practice of Design* class ended at 5:00 p.m., but the December afternoon was accompanied by a darkened sky.

"We of all people know that we can't wait for things." I put the phone call on my headphones and continued.

"Everything can change instantly," I said.

I checked my exam schedule on my phone.

"Classes end on December 6th and my exam is December 16th; we can leave on the 7th and come back on the 13th so I have the weekend to study," I pleaded.

I knew this was a tight timeline, but I needed to go see Nonna Rina. I had an insistent instinct to see her as soon as I was able to. Nonna Vittoria had died five months prior and I missed her fiercely. I wanted to be close to Nonna Rina.

"We have to go," I said. "I don't want to wait until April."

AFTER HANDING IN MY *COMMUNICATING IN A WORLD OF DATA* PORTFOLIO AND WORKING ON MY OTHER ASSIGNMENTS DURING THE DAY, I AR-RIVED AT PEARSON AIRPORT FOR OUR 9:00 P.M. FLIGHT.

My printed lecture notes for my *Human Perception and Commu-nication* exam, laptop, and week-long essentials in my carry-on bag weighed on my shoulder, as I walked through Terminal 3 to meet Mom. She greeted me with a hug and an extra rolling carry-on for me to fill. After transferring my belongings to the rolling carry-on, Mom and I made our way through security and to the gate.

We boarded the sparsely occupied plane. After the remaining passengers boarded, Mom went to sit in the row of vacant seats in front of me. I remained in my designated seat. I pulled out my lecture notes but quickly traded them for my headphones and the *All Out 70s* playlist on Spotify. I waited for take-off.

Mom and I were held on the plane for five hours before we were finally told that the plane had engine problems that couldn't be fixed. Our hearts fluttered each time the flight attendant would give us an update, only for it to turn into an extended delay, and ultimately, defeat. We needed to exit the aircraft and try again the next day.

AFTER A LONG, DELAYED JOURNEY, MOM AND I ARRIVED IN ROME.

We walked to our apartment, passing the Christmas lights, Blu Bar Val Melania, and the cars parked on our one-way street.

I opened the door to our apartment and put my luggage on the floor. I walked into my childhood bedroom that Papà stayed in when he was dying. The bunk beds that we both laid on were now sawed in half and positioned on the floor. We called Nonna Rina to tell her we arrived and that we would rest today and see her tomorrow. Mom and I recovered our jetlagged-aching bodies.

The next day, Zio Claudio came to pick Mom and me up to bring us to Nonna Rina's home. We walked through the apartment courtyard filled with green shrubs and tall Stone Pine trees. Zio unlocked the doors to Nonna's building.

Nonna Rina was inside her apartment, waiting for us, her hand holding the weight of the open door.

She hugged me tightly. I held her a little longer than usual.

The same framed photos of me, Chiara, Papà, Giorgia, Federica, and Nonno Peppe filled her hallway when we entered. We sauntered to her sewing room.

Mom and I sat on the pull out couch facing Nonna and the big window facing her courtyard. A painted portrait of Papà wearing a green shirt against a purple background hung on her wall.

Plastic bags filled with her neighbours' garments laid on the floor waiting to be altered.

I showed her my first published article in *The Medium*—UTM's newspaper. She teared up at the sight of her and Papà's last name, Cassuoli.

"Che bel nome," she said, saying how beautiful our last name was.

Her forehead scrunched and tears fell from her squinted eyes.

Her face always lit up when she saw me on our Facetime calls. Her eyes always welled up when she saw me in person.

Nonna Rina wrapped me in her arms and told me how much I reminded her of Papà, how I'm all she has left of him. She put the newspaper on her bookshelf.

We talked about my plans to live in Rome after I graduated, so I could spend more time with her. I'd find a journalism job at *Il Messaggero* and visit her after work, or maybe write another book and move into her unoccupied, old family home in Mugnanese.

I loved Nonna Rina dearly but was never given the chance to have her as a physical constant in my life.

ON APRIL 5TH, 2020, ZIO CLAUDIO CALLED MOM TO TELL HER NONNA RINA WAS IN THE HOSPITAL IN GRAVE CONDITION.

She had a heart aneurysm. They couldn't stay with her because of the COVID-19 pandemic.

On April 6th, she died alone.

Not only could I not be there during Nonna Rina's last breath, but nobody could have been because of the circumstances. I can't be there now with Zio Claudio, Zia Patrizia, Giorgia or Federica to console them. They can't hold a funeral for her. They can't be close to each other during this devastating time.

I treasure the FaceTimes, the calls, and the cross-ocean-love that Nonna Rina and I had for each other, but being there as a physical constant is something that I was never able to do for her. Now, that opportunity has been stripped away from me.

They say that just because someone isn't physically there with you doesn't mean they're not there with you at all; but I never had the chance for that physicality with Nonna Rina.

The world has stopped because of the pandemic, but the deaths continue. The three deaths in three years that I have endured has turned into four deaths in four years.

After writing this book and processing my grief, I now have to restart the process. Grieving is never-ending, but for me, anytime there's progress it feels like I get hit with it again. I'm in shock. I'm numb. The turbulence of the water came full force again. I fell off my life raft. My body is heavy and I'm sinking.

I didn't see Nonna Rina often. In a way, it doesn't feel much different at this moment, because she's not someone I talked to or saw every day; but I know things will be different because my heart hurts. My heart is heavy.

I know one day I'll go reach out to phone her but then remember that I no longer can. I'll no longer be able to see her face light up on FaceTime or hear her voice change from monotone to pure excitement when she answers her phone and says,

"*Pronto?*"

"*Ciao Nonna è Sara,*" I'd reply, telling her it's me.

Her voice would shift to pure joy—a higher tone and a louder volume.

Though I've been surrounded by so many deaths and people dying, I still don't know where somebody goes when they die. But Nonna Rina, I hope that wherever it is, you'll be reunited with Papà again. I hope that you can hold Nonno Peppe. I hope Nonna Vittoria makes you her homemade sauce, and Nonno Carlo pours you a glass of red wine. I hope you get to embrace Chiara.

I hope you know how much I love you.

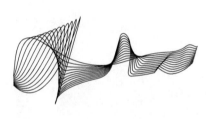

thank you and acknowledgements

Mom—I want to thank you for always answering my frantic calls. Thank you for helping me tell my story. Thank you for your constant, unwavering support in everything I do.

Jinder Oujla-Chalmers, Momo Yoshida, Robert Price, Guy Allen—thank you.

I want to acknowledge the people that I've met during my time at Etobicoke School of the Arts and University of Toronto.

Thank you to all teachers, students, peers, and friends who have helped me realize and nurture my intentions and goals.

Thank you to everyone reading this. Thank you for allowing me to tell, and try to make sense of, my story. Thank you for listening.

about the author

Sara Margherita Cassuoli Davide is an Italian Canadian writer. Her grandparents immigrated to Canada from Rome in 1955. She was born to an Italian father and Italian Canadian mother. She takes pride in her Italian heritage.

Sara Margherita is a new writer with a passion to express herself creatively and in any way she can.

Though she has dealt with great losses since an early age, Sara Margherita always tries to bring positivity into the world and come from a place of passion and creativity.

When Sara Margherita is not writing, she is singing, playing piano, painting, or working on graphic design.

Her life experiences mould her writing, and her matter-of-fact tone and poetic imagery blend together in her voice as a new writer.

Manufactured by Amazon.ca
Bolton, ON